Bristol
Year Round

Spring, Summer, Autumn & Winter

Nigel Vile

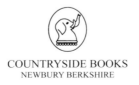

COUNTRYSIDE BOOKS
NEWBURY BERKSHIRE

First published 2020
© 2020 Nigel Vile

Reprinted 2022

COUNTRYSIDE BOOKS
3 Catherine Road
Newbury, Berkshire

To view our complete range of books,
please visit us at
www.countrysidebooks.co.uk

ISBN 978 1 84674 390 0

*All materials used in the manufacture of this book
carry FSC certification*

Produced by The Letterworks Ltd., Reading
Typeset by KT Designs, St Helens
Printed by Holywell Press, Oxford

Introduction

There is no doubt that particular walks do suit particular seasons. Spring is the season of new birth, with a rich array of wild flowers bursting forth and the sound of birdsong filling the air. What could be better than a woodland walk with a carpet of primroses, bluebells, wild garlic and wood anemones? Summer is the season of blue skies where walking on open hilltops is particularly apt. It is also the season of wild orchids and trefoil, knapweed and oxeye daisies – flora that in turn attracts vast numbers of butterflies. Autumn, that season of mists and mellow fruitfulness, is a glorious burst of colour with the reds and yellows, browns and oranges of our woodland cover. And winter is the time for a bracing walk along the shoreline of our coasts and estuaries, with a cosy pub and the warmth of a log fire to welcome you.

The Bath and Bristol area offers a range of landscape types, including the limestone upland of the Mendips and the contrasting lowland of the Somerset Levels. There is shoreline along the Severn Estuary and the

Bristol Channel, whilst the Avon Valley offers delightful riverside walking. And not to be overlooked are the Southern Cotswolds with villages crafted of golden limestone, ancient churches and drystone walls.

Here we have a collection of walks for each season of the year. Spring takes us to a carpet of bluebells in Leigh Woods and also the springtime flora and fauna of Hawkesbury Upton in the Cotswolds. In the summer, there is a seaside stroll at Sand Bay, as well as an upland walk at Lansdown, the scene of a Civil War battle in July 1643. Autumn colours are on display at Westonbirt Arboretum, as well as at Ashton Court with its deer park, whilst the winter season sees an atmospheric walk along the banks of the Severn with its wintering wildfowl, as well as a visit to the Somerset Levels and a chance to see the iconic starling murmuration.

It remains for me to wish you many hours of happy walking in this delightful part of the country with this collection of walks for all seasons.

Nigel Vile

Publisher's Note

We hope that you obtain considerable enjoyment from this book; great care has been taken in its preparation. Although at the time of publication all routes followed public rights of way or permitted paths, diversion orders can be made and permissions withdrawn. We cannot, of course, be responsible for such diversion orders and any inaccuracies in the text which result from these or any other changes to the routes, nor any damage which might result from walkers trespassing on private property.

The simple sketch maps that accompany the walks in this book are based on notes made by the author whilst surveying the routes on the ground. They are designed to show you how to reach the start and to point out the main features of the overall circuit, and they contain a progression of numbers that relate to the paragraphs of the text.

However, for the benefit of a proper map, we do recommend that you purchase the relevant Ordnance Survey sheet covering your walk.

We are anxious that all details covering the walks and the pubs are kept up to date and would therefore welcome information from readers which would be relevant to future editions.

Clifton Suspension Bridge

1 Leigh Woods and the Avon Gorge

4 miles (6.4km)

WALK HIGHLIGHTS

No spring is complete without a walk through woodland carpeted with bluebells. Leigh Woods on the fringes of Bristol fits the bill perfectly. Walk this way in springtime and you will also find primroses and flowering wild garlic, cuckoo pint and violets. This National Nature Reserve is also home to two plants found nowhere else in Britain – the Bristol Whitebeam and the Bristol Rock Cress.

Below the woodland lies the River Avon, at this point both tidal and navigable. Commercial traffic, however, is virtually zero since the port facilities in the heart of Bristol were officially closed in 1971. Shipping activity is now concentrated at Avonmouth, where the river joins the sea after its 75-mile journey from the Southern Cotswolds. Here in the Avon Gorge, with its cliffs rising over 200 feet above the river, we find Brunel's iconic Clifton Suspension Bridge, arguably Bristol's most recognisable landmark.

spring

HOW TO GET THERE AND PARKING: Take the A369 Bristol to Portishead road from Ashton Gate. Shortly after the traffic lights where the B3129 turns off to Clevedon, a sign on the right indicates the entrance to Leigh Woods. Follow a drive called Coronation Way for ½ mile to a parking area on the right. Continue for another 225 metres – the drive bears left – to reach the main Leigh Woods car park. **Sat Nav:** BS8 3QB.

MAP: OS Explorer 155 Bristol & Bath. **Grid ref** ST553741.

TERRAIN: Woodland tracks and a path with a firm surface alongside the River Avon. One climb through Nightingale Valley.

FOOD & DRINK: There are no refreshment facilities on the walk, so bring along a picnic to enjoy in the woodland. The nearest pubs and cafés are a 5-minute drive away in Clifton. Try the **Albion** at Clifton, BS8 4AA. ☎ 0117 973 3522 ⊕ thealbionclifton.co.uk

THE WALK

1 Follow what becomes a track at the far end of the car park signposted to **Paradise Bottom**. In 350 metres, having passed **Oakwood Lodge** on the left, continue following the track beyond a barrier. In ¼ mile, at a junction by a telegraph pole, continue ahead for 200 metres to the next junction. Turn right on a path signposted to **Pill** and drop down to the **River Avon**. Along the way, you will see the best bluebell displays on the walk.

2 Turn right and follow the **Avon** upstream for almost 2 miles. Here the river is navigable and you could well see pleasure boats on the water. About 150 metres before the path passes under the **Clifton Suspension Bridge**, turn right under a railway bridge to follow a public footpath into **Leigh Woods**. This is a truly spectacular section of the walk as the river carves its way through the **Avon Gorge**. Increasingly, Brunel's **Suspension Bridge** begins to be a dramatic backdrop.

3 Follow the woodland path uphill through **Nightingale Valley**. This is the only ascent along the way but the woodland provides welcome shade.

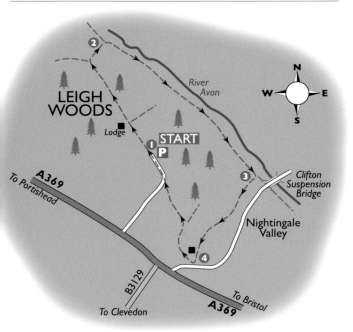

It is here that you might spot the Bristol Whitebeam or the Bristol Rock Cress. In ½ mile you come to a path on the right, shortly before the B3129.

Follow this path gently uphill to the right to a clearing. Turn left and walk up the left edge of this clearing to a handgate by some properties. Beyond this gate, follow the path through a **National Trust Ranger Base** to reach the line of a wall. In 100 metres, by a gate, turn left through a gap in the wall to follow a path signed as '**National Cyclepath 41**'. In ¼ mile, on reaching **Coronation Way**, turn right, back to the car park.

spring

The view from Solsbury Hill

2 Solsbury Hill
3 miles (4.8km)

WALK HIGHLIGHTS

Solsbury Hill, immortalised in Peter Gabriel's song of the same name, is the perfect spot to walk in late spring. The hilltop is awash with buttercups and clover, whilst from high above in skies full of white fluffy cumulus clouds comes the sound of the skylark.

Below lies Chilcombe Bottom, site of a reservoir in a former life but now a wetland nature reserve. In late spring, yellow flag and marsh marigold abound around the water's edge, whilst the signs warning of adders possibly enjoying the first real sun of the season should be heeded.

The woodland above Chilcombe Bottom appears snow-covered, but this is simply flowering wild garlic. This is a perfect time of year for some

spring

HOW TO GET THERE AND PARKING: From the large roundabout on the eastern edge of Bath where the A46 meets the A4, follow the signposted local road into Batheaston village. In the centre of Batheaston, follow a minor road signposted to Northend and St Catherine. In 550 metres, park on the roadside as close as possible to a left turn called Seven Acres Lane. **Sat Nav:** BA1 7HE.

MAP: OS Explorer 155 Bristol & Bath. **Grid ref** ST779683.

TERRAIN: Quiet lanes and footpaths with one relatively steep climb onto Solsbury Hill.

FOOD & DRINK: There are no refreshment facilities on the walk. Solsbury Hill, however, is a perfect place for a picnic. Back in Batheaston, try the **Gather Café** ☎ 01225 851494. No website.

early season foraging in an amazingly rural landscape so close to the heart of Bath.

THE WALK

Walk up **Seven Acres Lane** and, at the top of a climb, keep on the road as it bears right to soon pass **Chris Rich Farm Shop**. Beyond this shop, keep on the lane as it bears left and continue for ½ mile to a drive on the right leading to **Chilcombe House**. Ahead is a small stone building – climb the steps to the right of this building into **Chilcombe Bottom Reserve** and follow the path to the right of the former reservoir and onto a gate by a property.

Turn right and follow what soon becomes an enclosed track through the valley to a gate. Continue along an enclosed track to reach a derelict barn on the left. Pass through a gateway immediately after this barn and head across the field ahead, climbing uphill and following the line of an electricity power line, to reach a stile at the top of the climb. Beyond this stile, turn left and follow the left edge of a field along to a gate at the far end of the field. Continue along a section of enclosed path to the next gate before climbing uphill onto the common land of **Solsbury Hill**. Keep ahead onto the hilltop, turn right and walk around to the trig point with its commanding view. The views extend

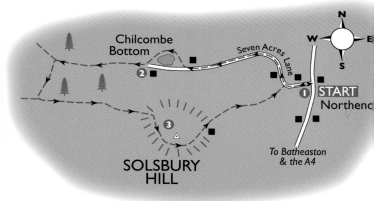

from the Wiltshire Downs above Cherhill to Bath and the more distant Mendip Hills.

3 Continue walking around the edge of the hilltop, passing a farm below on the right, and continue around to the north-eastern corner of the hilltop. Towards the corner of the hilltop, look out for a property below on the right by a telegraph pole. At this point, drop downhill on a rough path to reach a track by the house. Turn left and, immediately past the property, pass through a handgate on the right and drop downhill in the field ahead to a gate in its far corner. This field is a riot of colour in springtime, when awash with traditional English flora. Walk down the left edges of the next two fields to reach a market garden. Walk down the left edge of the market garden to reach a gate and **Seven Acres Lane**, before dropping downhill back to the main road in Northend.

spring

Harptree Combe

3 East Harptree
4½ miles (7.2km)

WALK HIGHLIGHTS
East Harptree Combe, a secluded and wooded valley, is a particular delight during springtime. The woodland is carpeted with bluebells and wild garlic flowers, whilst earlier in the season primroses lend this delightful spot shades of yellow.

Deep in Harptree Woods lies what remains of the East Harptree Leadworks, most notably the Smitham Chimney and a small reservoir. The water here is teeming with life during the spring, from newts to dragonflies.

THE WALK
Starting by the **Community Shop**, continue following **Whitecross Road** for 275 metres to a stile and footpath on the right, immediately past an orchard and passing a right turn – **Water Street** – along the way. Cross this stile, and follow the right edges of three fields to a stile and lane alongside some properties. Turn left then immediately right following a side lane for 550 metres up to a detached property. Follow the track to the left of this property for 150 metres and, where this track ends, pass through a handgate on the right and enter a hillside field. Head uphill to a gate in the top field boundary just past an isolated tree and, in the following field,

11

spring

HOW TO GET THERE AND PARKING: Leave the A368 in West Harptree and follow the B4114 for ¾ mile before turning into East Harptree's High Street. In ¼ mile, at a junction by a clock tower, turn left into Whitecross Road and park on the roadside by the Community Shop. **Sat Nav:** BS40 6AA.

MAP: OS Explorer 141 Cheddar Gorge & Mendip Hills West. **Grid ref** ST567559.

TERRAIN: Quiet lanes and footpaths, with a climb up to Harptree Woods. East Harptree Combe can be muddy and the stream may have to be forded.

FOOD & DRINK: The Waldegrave Arms, BS40 6BD. ☎ 01761 206859. ⊕ thewaldegrave.co.uk.

head to a stile in the fence opposite, passing to the right of a telegraph pole. Beyond this stile, walk ahead to a stile in the hedgerow opposite. Cross the next field to a gate in the opposite field boundary and a track.

2 Turn right and follow this stony track uphill for 300 metres to a gate and footpath on the right, marked with a **Monarch's Way** marker, ignoring a slightly earlier gateway on the right. Follow the right edge of this field to a gateway opposite and, in the next field, head across to a stile, almost in the far left-hand corner. Beyond this stile, follow the left edge of the next field to a gate and track, before continuing for 250 metres to a road junction just above **Nettwood Farm**. Turn left and follow the lane for 150 metres, before taking a right turn into **East Harptree Wood**.

3 Follow the drive ahead and, where this drive bears left into a parking area, keep ahead along a gated track. In ¼ mile, on a left-hand bend, turn right along a waymarked path to **Smitham Chimney**. Keep on this path as far as a junction alongside the chimney at the western end of a pond. At this junction, turn right and follow a path behind the chimney and continue downhill to an exit gate from the woodland in 150 metres, ignoring a slightly earlier left turn. Beyond this stile, follow a track down past a farm complex on the left for 150 metres before turning left along a track just before a property and a road to reach a gate and field.

4 Cross to a gate in the middle of the end field boundary. In the next field, drop downhill to a gate in the bottom right corner, bear right to a second gate and turn left to drop down the left edge of the adjoining field to a gate and lane. Turn left and, in 50 metres, pass through a handgate on the right before walking across the bottom of a field to a gate at the entrance to **Harptree Combe**. Follow the path through the combe for ½ mile until it bears right

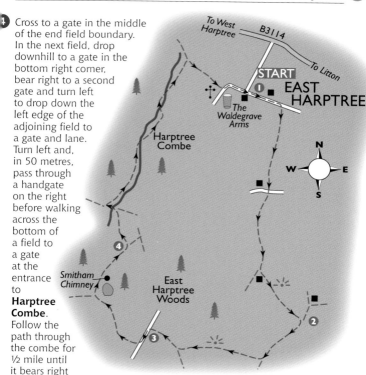

and drops down to a junction. Keep left, and continue following a stream down through the combe, passing beneath an aqueduct, to reach a gate and stile in 500 metres. Cross this stile at the end of the wood, turn right and follow a grassy track in the corner of the field to a stile. Walk across the field ahead to a stile by **East Harptree church** before following a path to the road by the pub. Follow the road to the left around to the centre of the village.

13

spring

View of the Severn Vale

4 Hawkesbury Upton

5½ miles (8.8km)

WALK HIGHLIGHTS

The Cotswolds provides excellent walking throughout the year, but arguably shines brightest in spring. The fields and hedgerows are bursting into life with a rich array of flora and fauna, whilst the woodlands are carpeted with bluebells and primroses. Overhead, the skylark will be impressing with its flight and song, whilst the good visibility at this time of year will mean fine views across the Severn Vale towards the Forest of Dean and the distant Welsh hills.

It is not just natural history on this walk, however, but also human history. There is the Somerset Monument, commemorating Lord Edward Somerset, born at nearby Badminton, who led the British cavalry at the Battle of Waterloo, and there is also Horton Camp Hillfort, high on the hilltop above Horton Court.

THE WALK

1 Turn left out of the village hall car park toward the **Beaufort Arms** before turning right into the pub's car park. Pick up a footpath in the far

14

HOW TO GET THERE AND PARKING: Follow the A46 north from Bath to Petty France and Dunkirk before taking a left-turn signposted to Hawkesbury Upton. Having passed the Beaufort Arms, the Village Hall and its car park are on the right. Parking is free but there is a voluntary donations box. **Sat Nav:** GL9 1AU.

MAP: OS Explorer 167 Thornbury, Dursley & Yate. **Grid ref** ST777870.

TERRAIN: Quiet lanes, footpaths and tracks; one descent/ascent beyond Horton Camp Hillfort.

FOOD & DRINK: The Beaufort Arms GL9 1AU. ☎ 01454 238217. ⊕ beaufortarms.com.

right corner of the car park and continue ahead to an open field. Turn left, walk along to the corner of the field and turn right to follow the field boundary alongside a number of properties to a gate. Cross the next field to a gate opposite, cross a road and follow a track for ¼ mile to a point where it bears right to a barn. At this point, keep ahead across an arable field to reach an old wooden stile. Keep going, a field boundary on the left, to a gap in a wall. Continue ahead, walking up to and along the left edge of **Bodkin Hazel Wood**, to reach a track.

Turn right through a gateway and follow a path with **Bodkin Hazel Wood** on the right. Where the woodland ends, continue following the grassy path ahead for ½ mile to reach a lane. Turn left and, in ¼ mile, pass through a gate on the right to enter the **Iron Age Horton Camp Hillfort**. Walk across to a gap in the rampart before walking down to the bottom right corner of the hillfort enclosure. Turn right and follow a path – the **Cotswold Way** – along the left edge of a hilltop field to reach a handgate. Follow the path as it winds its way downhill through woodland to reach the next gate and a hillside field. Turn right and follow the path across the hillside to reach a gate in the corner of the field, all the while enjoying views of **Horton Church and Court** below.

Follow the path ahead for 40 metres through woodland to the second of two consecutive left turns, signposted the **Cotswold Way**. Beyond a

Bristol & Bath Year Round Walks

gate at the edge of the woodland, continue across an area of scrubland before following the **Cotswold Way** across the right edges of three fields to reach a track. Follow this track to the left for ¾ mile to a lane on the edge of **Hawkesbury Upton**, with fine views to the west across the Severn Vale. Turn right to a junction by the ancient **Drovers' Pool**, now sadly choked with weeds, before following the village's **High Street** to the right for 300 metres back to the car park.

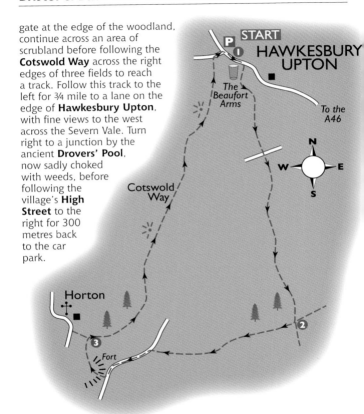

View towards Chew Valley Lake

5 The Chew Valley

5 miles (8km)

WALK HIGHLIGHTS

Chew Valley Lake is one of the region's best locations for fly fishing and birdwatching. Spring is a great time to visit, with an excellent chance of spotting ducklings, goslings and cygnets.

The walk also explores a section of the River Chew and the ascent of Knowle Hill, whose slopes are awash with bluebells at this time of year.

THE WALK

Leave the car park, turn right in front of the **Pelican Inn** and take the first right into **Tunbridge Road**. In ¼ mile, where the pavement ends, cross the road to a handgate opposite before walking up the left edge of a field to a gate. Keep ahead – it soon bears left – and drop down to a lane. Turn right then immediately left onto an enclosed footpath. Beyond a gate, follow a farm track past **Roundhill Farm** and down towards **Pitt's Farm**. Pass to the right of Pitt's Farm, keeping to the right of a wooden fence, before walking up the left edge of a field.

17

HOW TO GET THERE AND PARKING: Leave the A37 at Belluton, just north of Pensford, and follow the B3130 into Chew Magna. Just past the Pelican, turn left into the car park. **Sat Nav:** BS40 8SL.

MAP: OS Explorer 155 Bristol & Bath. **Grid ref** ST575631.

TERRAIN: Quiet lanes, footpaths and tracks; a gentle ascent onto Knowle Hill.

FOOD & DRINK: There is good pub fare at **The Pelican**, BS40 8SL ☎ 01275 331777 ⊕ butcombe.com/pubs/the-pelican. However, you may find it hard to resist the fish and chips while overlooking the lake at **Salt and Malt**, BS40 8XS ☎ 01275 333345 ⊕ saltmalt.com

2 Partway up the field, pass through a gate on the left and follow an enclosed path through to the flanks of **Knowle Hill**. Walk ahead for 150 metres before turning left to follow a faint path uphill to a seat on the summit of Knowle Hill. Follow a path behind the seat down to a lane, turn right and follow the lane around the flanks of Knowle Hill to reach **Knowle House** on the right in 350 metres. Continue following the lane ahead for 550 metres to a road junction, ignoring a left turn into **Hollowbrook Lane** and one other left turn along the way. Walk ahead to a junction, signposted to **Bishop Sutton**. Turn right along a cul-de-sac and continue for 200 metres to a gate and stile.

3 Beyond the stile follow a path on the right, almost doubling back on yourself. Follow this path along to a footbridge on the left, cross it and follow the path ahead, keeping close to **Chew Valley Lake**, to reach a car park. Cross the car park and continue along a lakeside path to another car park. Follow the exit road out, turn left and, having passed **Denny Lane** on the right, cross to a handgate opposite. Follow the right edge of a field to a lane, turn left and, just before a bridge, turn right and follow a path through woodland to a gate.

4 Cross the field ahead to a gate, before crossing a second field to a gate and footbridge. Turn right in a third field and walk across to a gate and footbridge, turn left and walk along to the next handgate, the Chew all the while on the left-hand side. Follow the left edge of the next field to a gate

18

in its corner, turn right along a track to a junction before turning left to a footbridge. Keep ahead to the bridge over the Chew before turning right on a path that climbs uphill to reach **Chew Magna's High Street**. Turn right and walk back to the centre of the village, turning right just before the **Pelican** back into the car park,

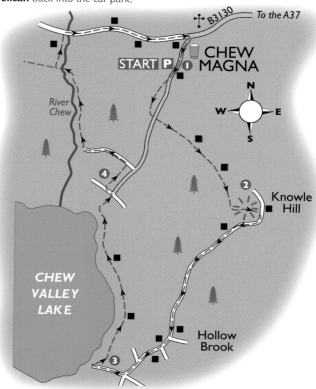

Priddy Nine Barrows and Ashen Hill Barrow Cemeteries

6 Priddy and North Hill

6 miles (9.6km)

WALK HIGHLIGHTS

High on North Hill above the village of Priddy are a series of mysterious round barrows known as the Priddy Nine Barrows and Ashen Hill Barrow Cemeteries. Excavations have revealed cremation burials and various grave goods such as beads, rings and spearheads.

Fieldpaths bring the walk to a high hilltop overlooking what appears to be all of Somerset, the Bristol Channel, West Wiltshire and a whole lot more. Beyond this lofty hilltop perch, an ancient drove track returns the walk to Priddy and the delights of the Queen Vic, a perfect place for a refreshing drink on a summer's day.

THE WALK

1. With your back to the telephone box, follow the main road to the left across the green, sheep hurdles on the left. In 300 metres, veer right

HOW TO GET THERE AND PARKING: Leave the A39 at Green Ore, 3 miles north of Wells, and follow the B3135 towards Cheddar. In 5 miles, turn onto an unclassified road leading into Priddy. Park on the far side of Priddy Green by a former telephone box. Sat Nav: BA5 3BB.

MAP: OS Explorer 141 Cheddar Gorge & Mendip Hills West. Grid ref ST527509.

TERRAIN: Quiet lanes, footpaths and tracks; a gentle ascent onto North Hill.

FOOD & DRINK: **The Queen Victoria**, BA5 3BA. ☎ 01749 676385. ⊕ thequeenvicpriddy.co.uk.

onto a side lane and walk up to **Priddy Church**. Follow a path to the left of the church down to a gate, cross a field to a gate opposite and continue ahead to a lane. Turn right and follow this lane for ½ mile to a handgate on the right just past a copse. Pass through this gateway and head across to the far-left corner of a large field, the far corner being initially beyond the brow of the hill and some 500 metres distant. As you approach the corner of the field, bear right and walk uphill to a group of round barrows on the skyline. Beyond these barrows, keep ahead across the field to a stile in the end field boundary.

Veer right in the next field towards a wall, **Priddy Nine Barrows** on the right, and follow the line of the wall across the hilltop to a stile. Enter the **Priddy Mineries**, an area of rough ground, and walk downhill keeping as close as possible to the boundary on the right. At a junction at the bottom of the hill by a beech tree, turn right and follow a path that borders a stream on the left. In 250 metres, cross a stile and a drive, walk through the grounds of the **Belfry Caving Club** to rejoin the drive and continue to a road by **Rose Cottage**. Turn right and, in 150 metres, having passed **Fair Ladywell Cottage**, pass through a handgate on the left and follow a path up the right edges of four fields to reach **Dursdon Drove**. Cross a stile opposite, slightly to the right, and follow the right edges of two fields to a stile and hilltop field with a panoramic view.

Turn right and walk along the right edges of two hilltop fields. In the corner of the second field, cross a stile on the right by a gate and water trough and follow the left edge of a field down to a gate. Drop downhill to a handgate and follow a path along to a driveway by **Higher Pitts Farm**. Follow the drive to Dursdon Drove, turn left and follow the track ahead for 500 metres to an enclosed path on the right with a **West Mendip Way** marker. Follow this path around to a stile, enter a field, turn right and walk up the right edges of two fields. In the top corner of the second field, turn left and walk along to a road. Turn right and follow this road into **Priddy**. At a junction a little way beyond the **Queen Victoria** pub, turn left back to the green.

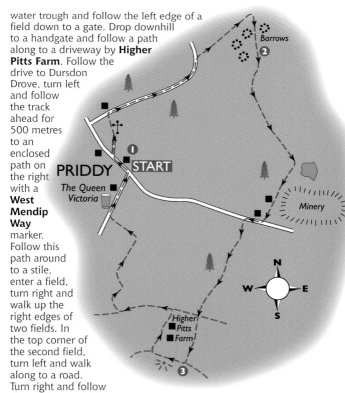

summer

Middle Hope

7 Sand Bay

5 miles (8km)

WALK HIGHLIGHTS

Summer would not be summer without a walk along the coast. This delightful walk explores the headland north of Weston-super-Mare, with a path that provides extensive views westwards towards the South Wales coast and the more distant Welsh hills.

This rocky headland is steeped in history. Archaeological excavations have revealed two Iron Age settlements, Romano-British pottery fragments and a 4th-century coin of the Valentinian period. Castle Batch, the mound just west of the trig point, is a Norman motte whose mound and ditch were unfortunately disturbed during wartime construction at the site.

summer

HOW TO GET THERE AND PARKING: Leave the M5 at junction 21 and follow the A370 towards Weston-super-Mare. Shortly, take a right turn signposted to Kewstoke and Sand Bay and continue for 3 miles through Weston's suburbs to reach the seafront road at Sand Bay. Follow this road to the right until it ends at a NT car park. **Sat Nav:** BS22 9UZ.

MAP: OS Explorer 153 Weston-super-Mare. **Grid ref** ST330659.

TERRAIN: Footpaths and tracks that cross an undulating landscape; the coast path is uneven in places.

FOOD & DRINK: The New Castle, Kewstoke, BS22 9YD. ☎ 01934 418417. ⊕ thenewcastle.co.uk.

There is also an abundance of birds that include not only seabirds but also swallows, greenfinches and skylarks.

THE WALK

1 Leave the car park, turn right and follow a path on the right signposted to **Middle Hope**. In 100 metres, turn left onto a stepped path and walk uphill to a gate and open hilltop. Turn right and walk along the right edge of the hilltop to a gap in a stone wall. Continue following the right edge of the hilltop towards another wall and, in the corner of the field, turn left and walk along to a gate on the right and a small walled enclosure. Pass through this enclosure and follow a track ahead alongside a wall to reach a metalled road. Cross this road and follow the path opposite, with a fence on your right, to another gap in a wall.

2 Continue to a gate on the right, where a short detour will enable you to visit **Woodspring Priory**. For the main walk, follow the middle of three paths towards a telegraph pole and continue to a metalled road and a disused MoD compound. Pass between a wall on the left and the fenced-in compound on the right to reach the **Bristol Channel coast**. Follow the coast to the left, the island of **Flat Holm** in the distance, keeping to a higher path at any junctions, to return to the small walled enclosure and gateway passed earlier in the walk.

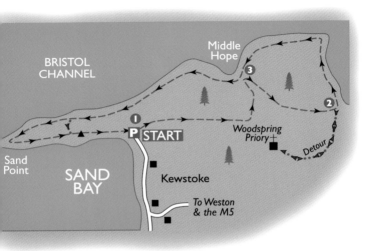

Keep ahead, passing above a cove known as **Middle Hope**. Continue along the edge of the coast for ½ mile until the path ends at a wooden fence and stile, cross the stile and climb uphill to the right to reach a junction in 150 metres. Two options remain. Either turn left and climb uphill to reach the hilltop and follow a path to the left along to a trig point. Beyond this point, follow a path to the right that drops downhill to return to the car park. Alternatively, for a more dramatic walk, keep ahead on the path and follow it until it reaches the end of the headland at **Sand Point**. Turn around and follow a rough stony path across the hilltop to the trig point before dropping downhill to return to the NT car park.

Litton's lower reservoir

8 Litton
6 miles (9.6km)

WALK HIGHLIGHTS

Tucked away in a fold in the Mendip Hills are a couple of hidden gems. Firstly, there is Hollow Marsh, traditional hay meadows offering glorious displays of wild flowers and orchids in summer, with swallows and skylarks overhead. The reserve is also home to quite literally tens of thousands of grasshoppers – but be sure to plan an early visit before the annual hay-making session in late summer.

Nearby are the Litton Reservoirs, created by damming the River Chew. These two lakes, built in 1850, are home to many wildfowl and offer far-ranging views across the Mendips.

summer

HOW TO GET THERE AND PARKING: Leave the A39 at Chewton Mendip between Bath and Wells and follow the B3114 into Litton. Park at the far end of The Litton pub's car park, by a horse chestnut tree. Non-patrons should park near the church, just off Litton Lane, and should start the walk from there. Sat Nav: BA3 4PW.

MAP: OS Explorers 141 and 142 Mendip Hills West & East. Grid ref ST595545.

TERRAIN: Footpaths, tracks and quiet lanes that cross an undulating landscape.

FOOD & DRINK: The Litton, BA3 4PW. ☎ 01761 241554.
⊕ thelitton.co.uk.

THE WALK

Drop down a stepped path by the chestnut tree to a road, cross and follow a second road to the right. In 100 metres, pass through a gate on the left and walk through **Litton's churchyard** to reach **Back Lane**. Turn right and, in 200 metres, left at a T-junction. In ½ mile, at a junction by the entrance to **Sherborne Farm**, turn right along a cul-de-sac before continuing along a bollarded footpath that shortly borders the infant **River Chew**. Continue along the path as it borders **Litton's lower reservoir** to reach a dam in ¼ mile. Cross the dam and follow a path to the right that borders the upper reservoir. In 700 metres, almost at the end of this reservoir, cross a stile in the hedgerow on the left and follow a path ahead across a field and a driveway before keeping ahead to reach **Shortwood Common**.

Walk across the common following a line of telegraph poles to reach a road and turn right. In 100 metres, turn right at a T-junction and follow the road ahead for 150 metres to a right-hand bend by a property. Turn left and follow a track known as **Hollow Marsh Lane** for 1 mile, ignoring a footpath on the right in ¾ mile, to reach a T-junction. Turn right and walk down to a gate at the entrance to **Hollow Marsh Nature Reserve**. Walk the length of this hay meadow and, at its far end, cross a stile and footbridge in the corner of the field to enter an uncultivated section of **Hollow Marsh**. Follow the left edge of this field to a stile in

27

the corner of the field before walking ahead through woodland. At the end of the woodland, ignoring a footbridge on the left, keep ahead into a field.

3 Cross this field to a gate, turn right passing through a gateway and follow the track ahead through **Chewton Wood** for ½ mile to a gate at the far end of the woodland, ignoring all side turns along the way. Turn left and follow a track uphill for 300 metres to a gate and stile on the right. Beyond this stile, cross the field ahead to reach a gate in its far right corner, before following a track for 700 metres to reach a road. Turn right and, in 200 metres, at a junction with **Shortwood Lane**, turn left. Turn right at the next junction and follow a road that winds its way through Litton to reach the stepped path on the left in 350 metres that leads back into the car park.

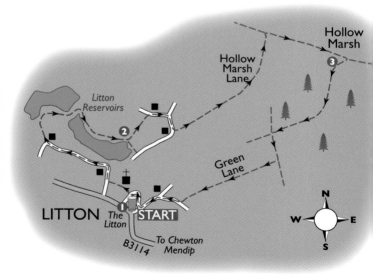

View of Swainswick Valley from the walk

9 Lansdown

3 miles (4.8km)

WALK HIGHLIGHTS

This walk looks across the Avon Vale towards the distant Mendip Hills, before Hanging Hill brings a view stretching across Bristol towards the distant Welsh hills. Finally, there is a view into the Langridge Valley and beyond towards Brown's Folly and Bathampton Down.

This is a particularly pertinent walk in summer as 5 July marks the anniversary of the Battle of Lansdown during the English Civil War. Hanging Hill marks a point where Parliamentary forces gathered against the eventually victorious Royalists.

HOW TO GET THERE AND PARKING: Follow the main road out of Bath up onto Lansdown Hill. Having passed the entrance to Bath Racecourse, take the right turn signposted to Langridge. Almost immediately, turn right and park in a layby alongside the main road. Sat Nav: BA1 9BX.

MAP: OS Explorer 155 Bristol & Bath. Grid ref ST725691.

TERRAIN: Footpaths and tracks that cross a gently undulating hilltop.

FOOD & DRINK: The Blathwayt Arms, BA1 9BT. ☎ 01225 421995. ⊕ blathwaytarms.co.uk.

THE WALK

1 Follow the main road to the left and, in 30 metres, turn right along an access road to **Bath Racecourse**. In 300 metres, just before some golf greens, turn right onto a bridleway. In 375 metres, at a junction, turn right and, in a few paces, turn left into woodland. Follow a path through the woodland, keeping to its left edge. In 200 metres, cross a driveway leading to **Brockham End** and continue following the path ahead. In 250 metres, at the end of the woodland, exit left onto a track by golf greens. Follow this track to the right and, in 100 metres, at the end of the golf course, veer right onto a footpath to a handgate.

2 Follow a path through conifers to a gate before following an enclosed path into a field. Follow the left edge of this field to a gate and **Hanging Hill** where the Parliamentary forces gathered in the Civil War all those years ago. Turn right and walk across the hilltop to a gate. Continue along a path to a driveway and turn right. In 50 metres, just before the entrance to the **Avon Fire and Rescue centre**, pass through a gate on the left and follow a path through an area of grassland to the next gate. Follow the road ahead around a bend on the left and, in 50 metres, turn left and pass through a belt of trees to reach the main road crossing **Lansdown**. Cross the road and follow a path opposite that bears left down to a **Civil War monument**. Pass to the right of this monument and drop down into some woodland, cross a stile and follow a path that eventually bears right up into a field, the site of the **Battle of Lansdown**.

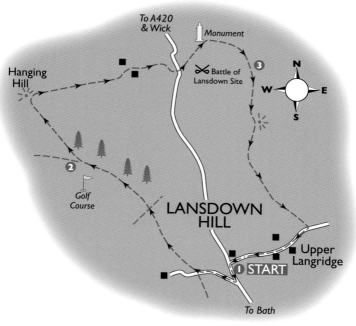

Walk down the left edge of this field to a stile, cross the stile and turn right along the hilltop to a gateway, with fine views to the left of the **Langridge Valley**. Follow the left edge of the next field to a gate, then, continue along the left edge of the following field to a gateway. Keep ahead, again following the left edge of the next field for 300 metres to a handgate on the left. Pass through this gateway and walk across the field ahead, bearing left all the while, towards a barn on the right. Pass the entrance to the barn complex, walk ahead to a telegraph pole and bear right over to a farm gate. Drop down a track to a lane in **Upper Langridge**, turn right and follow the lane for ½ mile back to the layby.

31

summer

10 Draycott Sleights

5 miles (8km)

WALK HIGHLIGHTS

Draycott Sleights is one of the less well-known beauty spots of the Mendip Hills, an area of unimproved limestone grassland with fine views across the Somerset Levels towards the Quantock Hills and Exmoor, the Bristol Channel and the Welsh Coast. This is altogether perfect walking country for a fine summer's day.

THE WALK

1 Facing the **Strawberry Special**, follow **Station Road** to the left before turning left into **Milking Lane**. In 300 metres, at a junction, turn right onto a track shown as **Dolemead Lane** on the OS map. In just under ½ mile, at a junction with **Latches Lane**, turn right and walk for ½ mile up to the A371, ignoring a right turn called Westfield Lane along the way. Cross the main road, the **Cider Barn** on the left, and follow the lane opposite towards the **Mendip escarpment**. In 150 metres, at a junction with **Top Road**, pass through a gateway opposite and follow an

32

HOW TO GET THERE AND PARKING: Follow the A371 into the centre of Draycott before turning south into Back Lane to reach a junction with Station Road. Turn left and park on the roadside by the Strawberry Special Inn. Sat Nav: BS27 3TQ.

MAP: OS Explorers 141 Cheddar Gorge & Mendip Hills West. Grid ref ST475507.

TERRAIN: One very steep climb of over 500 feet onto Draycott Sleights.

FOOD & DRINK: The Strawberry Special Inn, BS27 3TQ.
☎ 01934 742177. ⊕ strawberryspecial.com.
Closed at lunchtimes on Mondays, Tuesdays and Thursdays.

enclosed path to a field. Cross this field to a gate, walk up the left edge of the field ahead to a gate and stile on the left, immediately past some farm buildings.

Cross this stile, turn right and walk uphill to a stile at the top of the field. Climb uphill through **Batcombe Hollow** and, by a standing stone, bear right and follow a path that shortly bears left before climbing uphill to a gate at the top of the field beyond a standing stone and pond on the left. Beyond this gate, turn right and walk across to a gate in the right-hand field boundary, 100 metres up from the bottom corner of the field. Cross a track to a handgate opposite and enter the **Draycott Sleights Nature Reserve**. Bear half-left and follow a path that passes above a series of rock faces. In ¼ mile, towards the far end of these rock faces, bear right to a post and drop downhill to a gate in the bottom right corner of the field. Continue along a track to **New Road**.

Cross a stile opposite and follow the right edge of the reserve ahead along to an old stone barn, ignoring a right turn along the way. Keep ahead to the far side of the field and a gate and stile at the entrance to **Rodney Stoke NNR**. Drop downhill through woodland to a gate and field, before walking down to the bottom right corner of the field ahead. Cross a stile, follow a path down to a road just past a property called **Rose Mount** and turn right to reach the A371 in 350 metres.

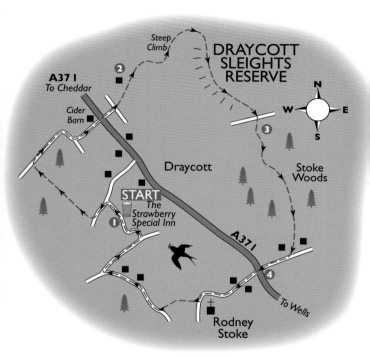

④ Cross and follow **Stoke Street** opposite to reach **Rodney Stoke's church** in ¼ mile. On a bend by the church, cross a stile and walk across the field ahead to a gate before crossing the next field to a stile in the wall opposite to join a lane. Follow this lane to the right to reach a road junction in 700 metres. Turn right, signposted **Draycott**, and continue to a junction by a small green in 650 metres. Turn left and, ignoring all side turns, follow the road as it winds its way back to the **Strawberry Special**,

34

Westonbirt Arboretum

11 Westonbirt
5 miles (8km)

WALK HIGHLIGHTS

The trees of Westonbirt Arboretum present a spectacular colour show in autumn, with leaves that have been green all summer turning to brilliant shades of yellow, orange and red.

Away from the Arboretum, this walk explores the undulating Cotswold plateau starting at Leighterton, a handsome village of stone cottages, quiet lanes and a pretty church just a few miles north of Bath.

autumn

HOW TO GET THERE AND PARKING: Follow the A46 north from Bath to Old Sodbury. Continue following the A46 for another 8 miles before taking the second of two right turns signposted to Leighterton. At a junction by the Royal Oak, turn right and drive down 'The Street'. Having passed the church, park on the roadside by a telephone box. **Sat Nav:** GL8 8UN.

MAP: OS Explorer 168 Stroud, Tetbury & Malmesbury. **Grid ref** ST824911.

TERRAIN: Virtually traffic-free country lanes, tracks and fieldpaths. Potentially muddy in places.

FOOD & DRINK: The Royal Oak, GL8 8UN. ☎ 01666 890250 ⊕ royaloakleighterton.co.uk.

THE WALK

1 With your back to the telephone box, follow **The Street** to the left. At a junction by a pond, keep on the road ahead signposted to **Didmarton**. In ¾ mile, having passed the entrance to **Park Wood Farm**, continue uphill for 100 metres before turning left onto a restricted byway. Follow this byway for ¼ mile to a lane and turn right. In 250 metres, with a restricted byway on the right, turn left onto a driveway. The walk all the while is crossing the undulating **Cotswold plateau**, a pleasant pastoral landscape.

2 In a few steps, turn right to a handgate and cross the field ahead to a gate on the far side of the field. Follow the left edges of the next four fields and, on entering a fifth field, turn left through a gateway to enter **Westonbirt Arboretum**. Follow the main track ahead for ¾ mile to a T-junction. Keep ahead, following a grassy path uphill to a gate at the edge of the Arboretum. Follow the bridleway ahead for 200 metres to its junction with a track in a shallow valley. Turn left along to a gate at the end of some woodland. It is imperative that you stick to the main track through the arboretum – deviate from its course and you could be charged for exploring the woodland on its private paths!

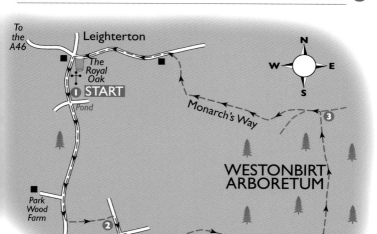

Walk ahead to a gate and stile at the end of the first field. Ignoring the gate and the track ahead, cross the stile and enter a hillside field. Bear half-right, walking uphill, to reach a point where a wall forms a corner. Immediately past this corner, turn right and follow the line of the wall down to a stile. Follow the right edge of the next field to a stile and enclosed path. Where the enclosed path ends, cross a stone stile on the right before turning left to walk across a field to a gate and road on the edge of **Leighterton**. Follow the road ahead, passing a cemetery on the right with a number of war graves, before reaching the **Royal Oak** in 350 metres. Turn left back to the church and your car.

12 Monkton Farleigh

4 miles (6.4km)

WALK HIGHLIGHTS

This is an autumn walk that has it all – ancient woodland with its colourful hues, opportunities for foraging, views across a mist-shrouded Avon Valley and stories of ghostly apparitions, particularly apt during this season.

The walk starts in Monkton Farleigh, the 'Monkton' a reference to the priory founded here in 1125. You can still see the Monks' Conduit, a small 14th-century building with a steep-pitched roof, standing all on its own in a field.

HOW TO GET THERE AND PARKING: Leave the A363 between Bathford and Bradford-on-Avon and follow an unclassified road signposted to Monkton Farleigh. In one mile, just before a road junction in the centre of the village, park on the roadside in the vicinity of the village school. **Sat Nav:** BA15 2QD.

MAP: OS Explorers 155 Bristol & Bath and 156 Chippenham & Bradford-on-Avon. **Grid ref** ST804654.

TERRAIN: Virtually traffic-free country lanes, woodland tracks and fieldpaths.

FOOD & DRINK: The Kings Arms, BA15 2QH. ☎ 01225 542469. ⊕ ourlocal.pub/pubs/the-kings-arms.

THE WALK

Walk along to the road junction in the centre of the village, turn right and walk down the village's main street. In 350 metres, just as you leave the village, turn left along a road signposted to **Kingsdown**. Keep ahead at a junction in 500 metres before taking the next left turn signposted to the **Blackberries Camping Park**. In 250 metres, turn left and follow a grassy path to a gate before keeping to the left edge of the field ahead to a gate and lane on the edge of **Monkton Farleigh**. Turn right and, in 100 metres, on a left-hand bend, keep ahead along a cul-de-sac lane to a gate and stile. Follow a tree-lined path – **Jubilee Avenue** – to a gate, stile and lane. Turn right and follow this lane for ¼ mile to business premises on the left.

In another 100 metres, pass through a gateway on the left and follow a waymarked permissive path through woodland to reach a gate and **Brown's Folly** in ¼ mile. Turn right and follow a path across the hilltop for 150 metres before passing through a gateway on the left and dropping down a stepped path to reach a hillside clearing. Turn left and follow the edge of this clearing across the hillside, with views below of the **Avon Valley**. At the far side of the clearing, veer right and drop down to a gate before following a woodland path across the edge of the hillside. Keep on this path for ½ mile until it reaches a junction with a path just below the boundary wall of the **Brown's Folly Reserve**. Here,

autumn

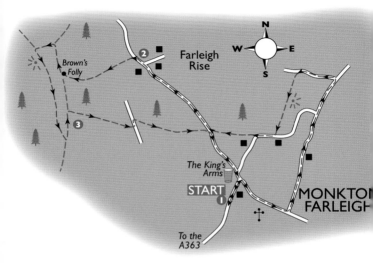

there is a marker post with both **Pepperpot Trail** and **Palladian Way** logos. Turn left and follow a path that runs along the top of the reserve, the boundary wall to the right.

3 In 600 metres, by a Brown's Folly Reserve information board, turn right and follow an enclosed path along to a gate. Follow the right edge of the field ahead towards some woodland. On the far side of the field, follow a track to the left into the woodland. In 25 metres, with a metal post on the left, turn right and walk through the trees to a lane just past a stone barn. Cross a stile opposite before following a path across the right edge of a field to a gate by some industrial buildings. Follow a track beyond this gate down to a gate and lane, before turning right to walk back to **Monkton Farleigh**. Just past the **King's Arms**, turn right on the road signposted to **Bradford-on-Avon** to return to the village school.

13 Ashton Court

2½ miles (4km)

WALK HIGHLIGHTS

When the trees change colour from those luscious summer greens to golden autumnal hues, and with a whiff of autumn in the air, where better to walk than through ancient woodland? On Bristol's doorstep is the Ashton Court Estate, with a deer park whose open spaces stand above Bristol's picturesque skyline of houses and harbour. The park is home to the 700-year-old Domesday Oak, chosen as one of the nation's 50 greatest trees to mark 50 years of the Queen being on the throne.

Ashton Court, with its massive 300-foot frontage, is an intriguing blend of styles ranging from Gothic and Jacobean to Tudor. This was home for

autumn

Bristol & Bath Year Round Walks

HOW TO GET THERE AND PARKING: Leave the A369 Bristol to Portishead road at Bower Ashton and follow Kennel Lodge Road along past the University of the West of England's Art College and through to the Ashton Court car park. **Sat Nav:** BS41 9JN.

MAP: OS Explorer 155 Bristol & Bath. **Grid ref** ST558719.

TERRAIN: An undulating landscape with one or two gentle climbs along the way.

FOOD & DRINK: The Courtyard Café, BS41 9JN. ☎ 0117 963 9176. ⊕ bristol.gov.uk/museums-parks-sports-culture/ashton-court-estate.

the Smyth family for over 400 years, with Thomas Smyth, an MP in Stuart times, being one of the last landowners to employ a jester. The family fortunes diminished during the 20th century and, in 1959, the whole estate was purchased by Bristol City Council for use as a public amenity.

THE WALK

1 Walk to the opposite end of the car park from **Ashton Court** and, where the road bears right, pass through a gap in the fence ahead and follow a gravelled path that bears left over to a gate at the entrance to **Ashton Court Deer Park**. Do not pass through this gate, instead turn left up towards some woodland. As the path enters the woodland, turn right and follow a path that winds its way uphill through the trees to reach a fence at the far end of the woodland. Turn left and follow the line of the fence as far as a gate on the right. Pass through this gateway, turn right and follow the fence bordering the Deer Park for 150 metres to a gate and a path coming out of the park. Turn left and follow a gravelled path for 50 metres to an estate road. Cross this road and continue following the gravel path ahead uphill for 350 metres to a fork.

2 Bear left down to an area of woodland, follow the main path ahead down to a T-junction and turn right. Follow this woodland path for ½ mile to a point where it bears sharply to the right and a side track drops downhill. Turn left down this side path and drop downhill to a T-junction. Turn left and follow a path that emerges from the woodland in 550 metres, with a

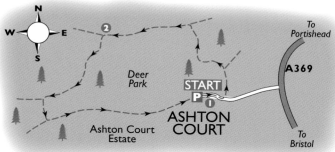

deer park on the left. Continue ahead along the main track for 300 metres to a junction and follow the estate road to the right. In 225 metres, walk across an area of grassland to reach **Ashton Court**. Pass through a gate on the right and follow a path along the imposing east-facing frontage of the mansion. At the far end of this path, pass through a gate back into the car park.

Becker's Wood

14 Castle Combe and the By Brook Valley

6 miles (9.6km)

WALK HIGHLIGHTS

The By Brook Valley offers some delightful ancient woodland, including a fine beech avenue in Parsonage Wood high above Castle Combe itself. Beyond the village there is also Becker's Wood, with various fungi and mosses as well as nature's bounty that is ripe for foraging.

    The picturesque village of Castle Combe, with its stone cottages, market cross and ancient bridge over the By Brook, is particularly atmospheric during the autumn when the season's mists mingle with the chimney smoke.

THE WALK

1 Leave the car park, turn right and right again at the next junction, walking downhill towards **Castle Combe**. In 300 metres, having passed the **Old Museum** on the right, turn left and walk uphill on a stony track. In 150 metres, take the second of two consecutive paths on the right, this one

44

HOW TO GET THERE AND PARKING: The visitors' car park in Castle Combe lies just off the B4039 Chippenham to Acton Turville road, some way out of the village. There is some roadside parking near the start of the walk just above the Old Museum, but this is fully used at peak times. **Sat Nav:** SN14 7HH.

MAP: OS Explorer 156 Chippenham & Bradford-on-Avon. **Grid ref** ST846777.

TERRAIN: An undulating landscape with a few moderate climbs along the way. Potentially muddy paths in the river valleys.

FOOD & DRINK: The Castle Inn, SN14 7HN. ☎ 01249 783030. 🌐 thecastleinn.co.uk.

opposite a stile on the left. Follow a woodland path for ½ mile to a gate and drop downhill to a junction and turn left. In 600 metres, just after the path enters woodland, follow a waymarked path on the right downhill. Shortly bear left and follow the path along to a footbridge.

Cross the **By Brook**, turn left and walk through the valley for ½ mile, crossing a footbridge along the way, to reach a handgate and track. Turn left into **Long Dean** and, at a crossroads by a letter box, turn left and follow a track for close on 1 mile back to the first junction passed on the walk. Keep ahead on the left-hand lower path and continue to a handgate. Follow a path by the By Brook to a bridge and join the road on the edge of **Castle Combe**. Turn left and, in 100 metres, veer right onto a path that climbs uphill into **Becker's Wood**.

Follow this woodland path for 650 metres to a stile and lane, turn right and follow the lane for ½ mile to a left-hand bend. On this bend, turn right onto a bridleway and follow this track for ½ mile down to a clapper bridge over the **Broadmead Brook**. Beyond this bridge, walk ahead to a handgate on the right, pass through this gateway and follow a path bordering the river for 500 metres along to **Nettleton Mill**. Turn right down to a semi-hidden handgate to the right of a double garage, before continuing to follow the Broadmead Brook until it emerges onto **Castle Combe Golf Course**.

autumn

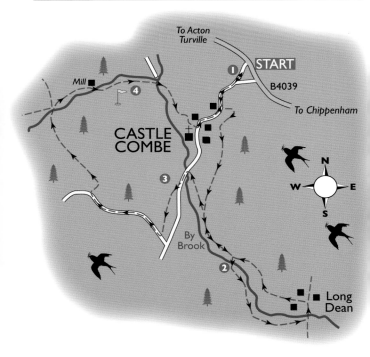

4 Follow a tarmac track to the right across the golf course to a bridge over the By Brook and a junction. Turn right on a metalled track and, in 50 metres, veer left onto a footpath. In 500 metres, partway through some woodland, pass through a gateway on the right and drop down some steps, pass under a bridge and join a back lane in Castle Combe. Follow this lane to the left, and shortly right, to emerge by the **Market Cross**. Turn left and follow a road back uphill to a junction in 600 metres, where a left turn leads back to the visitors' car park.

15 Mendip Heights

4½ miles (7.2km)

WALK HIGHLIGHTS

The Mendip Hills, famous for their limestone cliffs and caverns, reach their high point on Beacon Batch, above Burrington Combe. The geology here is quite fascinating – the original limestone anticline has been eroded on the hilltops exposing the underlying old red sandstone. This makes for a fascinating autumnal walk of great contrasts.

On the lower limestone slopes, there is traditional tree cover of ash and oak, sycamore and horse chestnut, with their seasonal hues of yellows, browns and reds. As the walk climbs onto the higher sandstone slopes of Black Down, there is a distinct change in vegetation to bracken and heathers, as well as bilberry plants, where the berries can be foraged

HOW TO GET THERE AND PARKING: Burrington Combe lies just off the A368, two miles east of its junction with the A38 at Churchill. Follow the B3134 road from the A368 for ½ mile to a parking area on the left. **Sat Nav:** BS40 7AT.

MAP: OS Explorer 141 Cheddar Gorge & Mendip Hills West. **Grid ref** ST476588.

TERRAIN: A walk onto Mendip's literal high point so expect some steep ascents, as well as an open and exposed hilltop.

FOOD & DRINK: The Plume of Feathers, BS40 7AH. ☎ 01761 462682. ⊕ plumeoffeathers.com.

in late summer and early autumn.

Just below Beacon Batch are a collection of barrows, whilst beyond the trig point, what appear to be a regimented series of ant hills are a series of mounds designed to make the invading Germans during the Second World War think that this lonely hilltop was in fact a street pattern resembling nearby Bristol.

THE WALK

1 From the car park, turn right and walk down past some public conveniences. In another 100 metres, turn right into **Ham Link**. In 200 metres, at a junction, keep ahead on a cul-de-sac lane signed as '**Unsuitable for Motors**'. In 200 metres, having passed a property on the left called '**The Hames**', pass through a handgate on the right into woodland. Follow the path ahead for 200 metres to a fork and marker post. Follow the left fork, a bridleway, and continue for 150 metres to a junction with a broad track. Follow this track to the left up onto the open ground of **Burrington Ham** and continue for 600 metres until the path drops down into a parking area by the B3134.

2 Turn left and follow the main road for 150 metres before turning right onto a track that initially passes **Ellick House**. Continue along this track until it emerges onto the open ground of **Black Down**. Walk ahead for 40 metres to a junction and marker post and turn left to follow a path along the eastern flank of Black Down. In ½ mile, at a junction, turn right onto

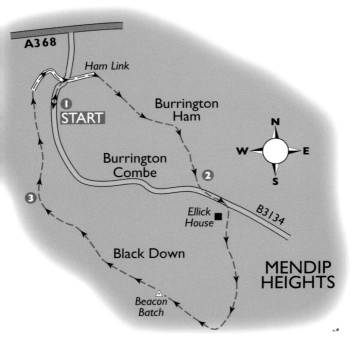

the first path on the right and follow this path uphill to the trig point at **Beacon Batch**. Beyond the trig point, follow the path ahead across **Black Down's ridge**. In 500 metres, at a fork, veer right and follow a path to reach a junction with a broad grassy ride in 325 metres.

Follow this ride to the right downhill to a cross track in just under ¾ mile. Keep walking ahead to a metal barrier and a junction with a track. Turn right through woodland to a cattle grid and continue along what becomes a lane down to the B3134. Turn right back to the parking area,

autumn

16 Tucker's Grave

4 miles (6.4km)

WALK HIGHLIGHTS

Following winter's heavy rain, fields and footpaths can often be impassable with the ground resembling little more than slurry. At times like that, a walk along quiet country lanes is the perfect answer, making this an ideal 'dry walk for a muddy day'. And this is a walk with an iconic starting point in the shape of Tucker's Grave Inn, arguably the country's best-known cider house.

HOW TO GET THERE AND PARKING: Tucker's Grave lies on the A366 two miles west of its junction with the B3110 at Norton St Philip. There is a parking area alongside the pub on the main road. **Sat Nav:** BA3 5XF.

MAP: OS Explorer 142 Shepton Mallet & Mendip Hills East. **Grid ref** ST752551.

TERRAIN: Virtually traffic-free country lanes that provide dry walking during winter's monsoon season.

FOOD & DRINK: Tucker's Grave Inn, BA3 5XF. ☎ 01225 962669. ⊕ tuckersgraveinn.co.uk. **The Faulkland Inn**, BA3 5UH. ☎ 01373 834441. ⊕ thefaulklandinn.pub.

In a former age, suicide victims were not permitted to be buried on hallowed ground so, when Edward Tucker hanged himself back in 1747, his body was buried at the side of a lonely crossroads in Somerset with his name being remembered by the local pub. Tucker's Grave is a unique cider house, with no bar and the pints being served from barrels in a bay window.

Those quiet lanes bring the walk to the village of Faulkland, a pretty place with a fine village green replete with a set of stocks opposite the local duck-pond. And tucked away along a back lane is Somerset Lavender, well worth a visit and open in November and December for Christmas shopping, even though the lavender fields are pretty dormant!

Once past Faulkland, more quiet lanes with a slight elevation bring far-ranging views towards Salisbury Plain, the Longleat Estate and the distant Mendip Hills.

THE WALK

Facing **Tucker's Grave Inn** from the parking lay-by, follow the road to the left. In 200 metres, keep ahead at a crossroads before continuing for 55 metres to a junction. Turn left and follow an unclassified road for a little over ½ mile to the A366. Turn right and walk through the village of **Faulkland**, admiring the village green with its stocks.

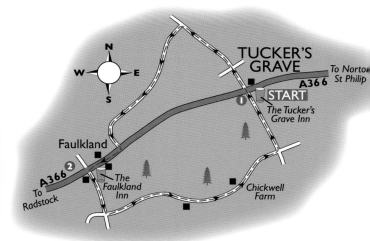

2 At a crossroads in 275 metres, by the **Faulkland Inn**, take the left turn towards **Hardington**. In 550 metres, at a crossroads, turn left and follow a quiet lane with far-reaching views across this corner of Somerset. In 1½ miles, at a crossroads, turn left towards **Faulkland** and **Wellow**. In 550 metres, this road reaches the legendary **Tucker's Grave Inn**.

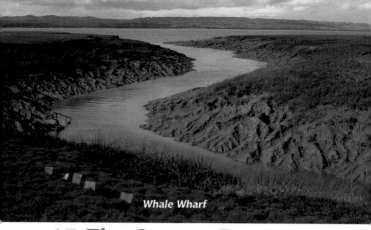

Whale Wharf

17 The Severn Estuary

6½ miles (10.4km)

WALK HIGHLIGHTS

The Severn Estuary supports many wading birds, perhaps 100,000 in a typical winter, searching eagerly for the ragworm, the lugworm and the hydrobia snails that thrive in its mudflats.

A key refuelling stop for migrating birds, the estuary sits on the North Atlantic Flyway, a bird migration route that stretches from Siberia across Europe and down to Africa. The Severn provides a vital service station where birds can rest and refuel. In the coldest of winters, wildfowl from more extreme parts of the UK also come south attracted by the warmer climate.

Over 2 miles of the coastal path alongside the Severn Estuary between Littleton and Oldbury are followed on this walk, as well as the countryside that borders the two villages.

THE WALK

With your back to the **White Hart**, follow the road to the right for 200 metres to a junction and small green. Turn right towards **Kington** and **Thornbury** and, in 225 metres, follow a turning on the left to **St Mary's Church**. Where this lane ends, continue across the right

HOW TO GET THERE AND PARKING: Leave the M48 at junction 1 by the First Severn Crossing and follow the B4461 towards Alveston and Thornbury. In two miles, in the village of Elberton, turn left onto an unclassified road signposted to Littleton-upon-Severn. The White Hart is on the right in 1¼ miles, just beyond a right-hand bend by the local village hall. There is a car park behind the White Hart for patrons. Alternatively, park on the roadside in front of Littleton's village hall. **Sat Nav:** BS35 1NR.

MAP: OS Explorer 167 Thornbury, Dursley and Yate. **Grid ref** ST597901.

TERRAIN: Virtually traffic-free country lanes, fieldpaths and tracks. There will be mud during winter months so appropriate footwear is vital.

FOOD & DRINK: The White Hart, BS35 1NR. ☎ 01454 412275 ⊕ whitehartbristol.com.

edge of the field ahead to a gateway in its far right-hand corner. Follow the right edge of a second field to a gate in its corner before following the right-hand edge of a third field. In the corner of this field, pass into an orchard. Head across to the far-right side of the orchard before passing in front of a cottage to join the road in **Cowhill**.

2 Follow the road to the left up to **St Arilda's Church**. Climb a path to a gate and the churchyard, walk around to the left of the church and enjoy the views across the estuary. Join a road on the far side of the churchyard, turn left and walk down past the village school for 200 metres to a footpath on the left – the **Severn Way** – just past the point where **Westmarsh Lane** comes in on the left. Follow this path through a complex of horse stables to reach a flood defence and the **Severn** in ¼ mile. Follow this flood defence, a raised grassy embankment, to the left for 1½ miles to an inlet known as **Whale Wharf**.

3 Having explored this muddy inlet, where a 68ft-long whale was stranded in 1885, pass through a handgate and continue following the Severn downstream for ¼ mile to a footpath marker sign on the

winter

left. Drop down to a gate and enter an open field. Walk across the field ahead to a stile in its opposite boundary before crossing a second field to a gate and stile. Beyond this stile, follow a track for ½ mile to the road in **Littleton** by the village hall. Turn left back to the **White Hart**.

winter

18 Bradford-on-Avon

3 miles (4.8km)

WALK HIGHLIGHTS

This is a perfect winter walk along the waterways between Bradford-on-Avon and Avoncliff. The outward leg follows the Kennet & Avon Canal where, on misty days, with wood smoke from the barges filling the air, there is a truly seasonal feel.

Moving along to Avoncliff, you will spot a vast aqueduct that carries the Kennet & Avon Canal across the River Avon, as well as the welcoming

56

HOW TO GET THERE AND PARKING: Bradford-on-Avon lies on the A363 between Bath and Trowbridge. In the centre of the town, just south of the Town Bridge that spans the Avon, is the railway station with its adjoining car park. **Sat Nav:** BA15 1EF.

MAP: OS Explorer 156 Chippenham & Bradford-on-Avon. **Grid ref** ST825607.

TERRAIN: Canal towpath and a tarmac riverside path. There should be little mud, but expect the occasional puddle on the towpath in the winter.

FOOD & DRINK: The Cross Guns, BA15 2HB. ☎ 01225 862335. ⊕ crossgunsavoncliff.com.

sight of the Cross Guns Inn with its roaring log fires. Constructed of the local Bath stone, there is prominent sagging on the centre arch of the aqueduct. But this actually occurred during the construction in 1798, and in no way signifies a dangerous structure!

Bradford-on-Avon, often referred to as 'Bath in miniature', needs little introduction. From the Town Bridge with its lock-up to the vast tithe barn, from the serried ranks of former weavers' cottages on the hillside above the Avon to a town centre dominated by small independent retailers, it is clear that this is a very special place.

THE WALK

Walk to the end of the station car park, drop down to the **River Avon** and turn left under a railway bridge. Walk across a grassy recreation area to reach a packhorse bridge on the right. Just beyond this bridge, veer left and follow a gravel path past a tithe barn and up to the **Kennet & Avon Canal**. Follow the towpath to the right – signposted to **Avoncliff** – for just over 1½ miles to reach the **Cross Guns** in Avoncliff.

Having enjoyed a rest at the Cross Guns, follow the towpath to the left back towards **Bradford-on-Avon** to reach bridge 173 in ¾ mile. Veer left and follow a tarmac path down into **Barton Farm Country Park**. Follow this path for ½ mile as it borders the Avon back to the packhorse bridge passed at the start of the walk. Retrace your steps across the

winter

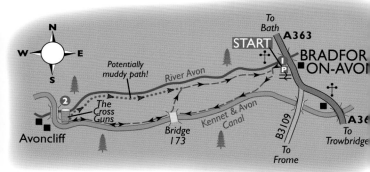

grassy recreation area back to the station car park before the inevitable exploration of Bradford-on-Avon itself.

> **Note:** *just as you leave Avoncliff for the return leg, there is a footpath on the left down to the River Avon whose bank can be followed to the tarmac path in direction point 2. In winter months, however, this path can be almost impassable due to its muddy condition.*

winter

Misty morning on a drove track

19 The Somerset Levels at Ham Wall

4 miles (6.4km)

WALK HIGHLIGHTS

Ironically, the winter months are often the best time to visit an area now termed the 'Avalon Marshes' by the tourist authorities, with seasonal mists lending the Levels a special atmosphere. It is also the time to catch the popular starling murmuration.

The murmuration occurs during the winter months because of the sheer numbers of starlings in the area at this time. Come the summer,

winter

HOW TO GET THERE AND PARKING: Leave the A39 Glastonbury Bypass to follow the B3151 towards Wedmore. In 3½ miles, in the village of Meare, turn left along a road signposted to Ashcott. In 1¼ miles, turn left into the RSPB Ham Wall car park. **Sat Nav:** BA6 9SX.

MAP: OS Explorer 141 Cheddar Gorge & Mendip Hills West. **Grid ref** ST448396.

TERRAIN: Flat terrain along the towpath, can be muddy.

FOOD & DRINK: The Railway Inn, BA6 9SX. ☎ 01458 741428. No website.

the birds head back to other parts of mainland Europe for the breeding season.

Ham Wall Nature Reserve is the focus of this walk, a fascinating wetland that was created when peat extraction ceased in the area. The reed beds and flooded workings are home to a rich array of wildlife that includes bitterns and otters, water voles and great crested newts, with the waterways containing a large population of eels. Easier to spot, and equally appealing, are the egrets and herons that stand as if sentries guarding the water's edge.

Note: the starling murmuration takes place in the hour or so leading up to dusk. If you can be at Ham Wall at sunrise, you will witness the flocks of starlings flying out of the reed beds on their daily quest for food.

THE WALK

1 Return to the road, turn right, cross the **Glastonbury Canal** and turn right to a stile. Beyond this stile, follow the path that runs alongside the canal for 1 mile to the second bridge that crosses the canal, detouring to the left along the way to visit the **Avalon Hide**. Cross the canal, turn right along a track – the former **Glastonbury Railway** – and, in 75 metres, turn left down to a gate and **Loxton's Marsh**.

2 Turn right and, in 80 metres, turn left and follow a grassy path for 200 metres to reach a hide. Continue along the path as it bears right and winds its way around **Loxton's Marsh**. In ½ mile, just below the track

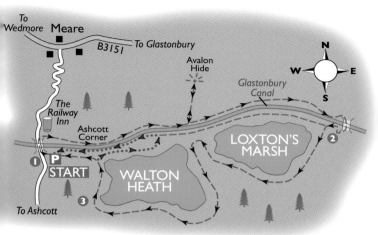

that marks the course of the old railway, turn left to a junction and a **Walton Heath Trail** signpost. Follow this path to the left for 550 metres before bearing right at a junction to a hide. Beyond the hide, follow the grassy path ahead – ignoring an early left turn that crosses a footbridge – to reach a junction in 200 metres.

Turn right and follow a path that runs around **Walton Heath** to reach a bridge on the left in ¾ mile. Detour along the cul-de-sac path to the right to find various hides – for the main walk, turn left and cross the bridge to rejoin the track that marks the course of the former Glastonbury Railway. Follow this to the left for 550 metres to a bridge that crosses the **South Drain**. Beyond this bridge, take the next left back into the car park.

winter

20 **Brean Down**

5 miles (8km)

WALK HIGHLIGHTS

There is nothing like wrapping up warm on a winter's day and walking along the coast. The waves will be ever more spectacular at this time of year, whilst a coastal walk will either relieve the stresses of the pre-Christmas period or provide the perfect way to unwind and walk off the excesses of the season and to confirm those New Year's resolutions about exercising more and eating more healthily!

Spectacular views are the primary attraction of Brean Down. Look

HOW TO GET THERE AND PARKING: Leave the A370 at Lympsham, 3 miles south of Weston-super-Mare, and follow an unclassified road signposted to Brean. On reaching the seafront road, turn right towards Brean Down and, in ¾ mile, turn left onto the Brean beach car park and park on the sands (fee payable). **Sat Nav:** TA8 2RS.

MAP: OS Explorer 153 Weston-super-Mare. **Grid ref** ST297576.

TERRAIN: A gentle stroll along a firm sandy beach before a steep ascent onto Brean Down, a rocky headland that protrudes into the Bristol Channel.

FOOD & DRINK: The National Trust Café, TA8 2RS. ☎ 01278 751897. ⊕ nationaltrust.org.uk.

west and there is the whole of the South Wales coast stretching from Newport to the Gower, encompassing Cardiff, Port Talbot, Swansea and the Mumbles. To the south lie the Quantock Hills and Exmoor, whilst to the east the Mendip Hills tower above the Somerset Levels.

Brean is one of those few places where visitors can actually park on the beach, so an added bonus is a gentle stroll along Brean Sands at the start and finish of the walk before the climb onto, and around, this rocky headland. This is a beach where dogs are welcome too, should you wish to give yours a day out at the coast. And for a shorter walk that excludes the Brean Sands section, drive along to, and park by, the National Trust shop at the end of the coast road where parking is free for members, and start the walk from that point.

THE WALK

Walk along the beach towards **Brean Down**, the rocky headland protruding into the **Bristol Channel**. In ¾ mile, at the end of the beach, turn right and walk up a ramp to reach a **National Trust shop and café**. Walk ahead to a road, turn left and continue to another tea shop. Beyond this tea shop, ignore the steps climbing uphill onto Brean Down, keeping on the road as it bears right. In 50 metres, bear left onto a path that climbs uphill onto the signposted Brean Down. Follow this path for 1 mile along the northern side of Brean Down, with fine views of **Weston Bay** below, to reach the western tip of this rocky headland. Cross a footbridge

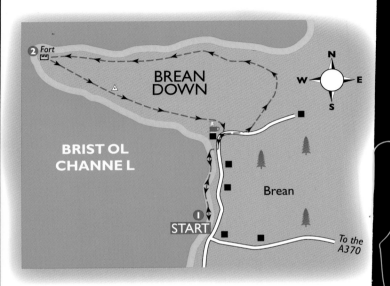

to explore the remains of **Brean Down Fort**, built to ward off a possible Napoleonic invasion.

2 Leave the fort by way of the footbridge, turn right and follow the line of a fence on the right. Where this fence ends, follow a grassy path uphill to reach a trig point in ¼ mile. Below all the while are fine views of Brean beach. Continue following the grassy path beyond the trig point for ¾ mile to a flight of steps on the right, just before another former military installation. Descend these steps, walk back to the National Trust shop and re-join the beach. Retrace your steps back to the car park,